THE CROWN

OR THE CLOWN

Your Season of Singleness

It's not about single and satisfied but single and whole!

"…Arise, go thy way: thy faith hath made thee whole."—Luke 17:19 KJV

LINDA A. DRUMGOOLE

ISBN 978-1-68526-709-4 (Paperback)
ISBN 978-1-68526-710-0 (Digital)

Covenant Books
11661 Hwy 707
Murrells Inlet, SC 29576
www.covenantbooks.com

"To Him who is able to keep you from stumbling, And to present you faultless before the presence of His glory with exceeding joy, to God our Savior, who alone is wise, be glory and majesty, dominion and power, both now and forever. Amen" (Jude 1:24–25).

To the women who, when I was called to preach the Gospel of Jesus Christ, the Word of truth, didn't push me away but embraced and mentored me: Evangelist Bernice Davis, Pastor Lisa Autry, Pastor Birdie Willis, and the incomparable (Bless God), Pastor Tonya McGill.

To the two women who wrote books by faith and inspired me: First Lady Doris Willis and Rev. Versinia Gooden.

To the one God gave to plant the seed, Princelle Wilson, who is within my Circle of Seven: Mary Drumgoole-Hammonds, Margaret J. Williams, Sandra Jacobs, Ethel Bowman, Valeria Johnson, and Vernita Tyler.

To my four: Bri, Pooh, Kendrick, and Marcs.

To my MSBC, KSBC, and BU Family (present and past).

To my family. (Are there any Drumgooles in the house?)

And to those who have gone on: Papa, Momma Rose, Mommie, Daddy, Roosevelt, and Larry.

TO YOU (too many to name)!

TABLE OF CONTENTS

PREFACE

Once upon a time, at a Christian Women's Conference far, far, away, a few of the circle of seven, Margaret, Ethel, Prince, and I sat together to receive a blessing. I was wowed by women who truly shared how they experienced their relationship with God. The conference addressed all areas of a women's life and spiritual walk in their faith. We then attended an open table discussion. Toward the end of the discussion, the moderator opened the floor to questions.

A question about singleness came up, and my eyes rolled back in my head. I thought if anyone makes that statement I was going to be done! Then a question was asked about mate choices. I thought, "Here it comes." The moderator pushed the one that posed the question to elaborate. During her explanation, she stated, "I want somebody who can make me laugh." Oh my goodness, I gagged! Some women began to make positive sounds of affirmation and clapped. I scoffed. I leaned toward my buddy Prince and snidely said, "Bobo, the clown can make you laugh!" She chuckled and simply remarked, "Write a book for these women." I laughed and thought, "Yeah, me write a book?"

Over 20 years later, God privileged me to minister to college-age and young professional women at the Morse Street Baptist Church (Where We Declare Jesus as Lord—Larry Willis, Senior Pastor). Almost daily, with broken or wounded hearts, they cried out to me about their heartfelt hurts, daunted desires and devastating disappointments. After almost each encounter, I could hear Prince's statement of "Write a book for these women." Yet, I still refused to write the book and would purposely push the thought away.

Then on October 2, 2018, my beloved brother, Larry Drumgoole, died. While at his home, on October 10, 2018, the same date my mother died in 2012, I began to write the book. Why? God moved! I pulled out my cellphone, into the note section, and I began first by typing the contents page. The Table of Contents reveals the dates I began writing each topic of this book. After returning home from the funeral, I began to write for each topic.

At that moment, the Lord immediately stripped me, took me to task, and activated my prepared heart, mind, and soul to give you "stuff." He tore it from me. I cried during the writing of this book. I became mad because of fresh emotions, unhealed pain, and renewed strength. I typed, stopped, and walked away from this book repeatedly. However, I returned repeatedly, wiped away tears, and began to write the book again and again. I felt transparent. I felt exposed but with the knowledge my testimony needed to be told to bless another, heal another, give strength to another…if only one. In the end, He restored, healed, and gave me joy unspeakable because of this book. I am completing the writing of this book as revealed by God for me…to you.

This book contains my words, my way, and my style. There are no errors or misspelled words. They are "My words. My way. My style." My editors (it's been edited dozens of times) would come to me repeatedly asking English teachers' questions about my sentence structure and word usage. I told them and I will share with you what I wrote from my heart, from experiences I went through or observations in my life. I used words and slang that flowed from my heart. I even made up a few words! Ha! Those work have a ^ (caret) in front of them. No errors…just honesty.

When gathering my thoughts for this book, I knew old suppressed feelings might resurface. They did! What did I do? I would stop and walk away from my calling to write this book. I would eventually return battered but better. During those times I walked away, I would cry huge tears and pray. I would go to my scriptures of strength and afterward spend time in worship. My peace returned and I would put on my "whole armor" and returned to where I left off. Why? It was because I laid that heaviness and pain before my God:

- ➢ Elohim (God)
- ➢ My Yahweh (Lord, Jehovah)
- ➢ My El Elyon (The Most High God)
- ➢ My Adonai (Lord, Master)
- ➢ My El Shaddai (Lord God Almighty)
- ➢ My El Olam (The Everlasting God)
- ➢ My Jehovah Jireh (The Lord Will Provide)
- ➢ My Jehovah Rapha (The Lord Who Heals You)
- ➢ My Jehovah Nissi (The Lord Is My Banner)
- ➢ My Jehovah Mekoddishkem (The Lord Who Sanctifies You)
- ➢ My Jehovah Shalom (The Lord Is Peace)
- ➢ My Jehovah Raah (The Lord Is My Shepherd)
- ➢ My Jehovah Tsidkenu (The Lord Our Righteousness)

Let me be transparent on what happened when I walked away. Prior to me reading that scripture of strength, worshipping and putting on my armor, I would make excuses about my unworthiness to write this book. Unworthy would be my cry of guilt and shame. However, during that rant with tears falling, I felt His Presence and only then did the peace come. I remembered *"I will lift up my eyes to the hills—From whence comes my help? My help comes from the LORD, Who made heaven and earth. He will not allow your foot to be moved; He who keeps you will not slumber. Behold, He who keeps Israel Shall neither slumber nor sleep. The LORD is your keeper; The LORD is your shade at your right hand. The sun shall not strike you by day, Nor the moon by night. The LORD shall preserve you from all evil; He shall preserve your soul. The LORD shall preserve your going out and your coming in From this time forth, and even forevermore."* — Psalms 121 (NKJV). My reply would be songs of worship.

My hope and prayers are that the words in this book would lead you to The Only One who heals and sustains. An ordained relationship ensures peace. Through that relationship, hope is established or restored and joy unspeakable and full of glory comes. I love each of you. Hold up! Don't tell me I can't love you. I don't know you, so how can I just use those words? But I do. (My words. My way. My style.) I love you unconditionally in the Lord. Blessings!

FOR YOU THROUGH THE WORD OF GOD.

Now Moses was tending the flock of Jethro his father-in-law, the priest of Midian. And he led the flock to the back of the desert, and came to Horeb, the mountain of God. And the Angel of the LORD appeared to him in a flame of fire from the midst of a bush. So he looked, and behold, the bush was burning with fire, but the bush was not consumed. Then Moses said, "I will now turn aside and see this great sight, why the bush does not burn." So when the LORD saw that he turned aside to look, God called to him from the midst of the bush and said, "Moses, Moses!" And he said, "Here I am." Then He said, "Do not draw near this place. Take your sandals off your feet, for the place where you stand is holy ground." Moreover He said, "I am the God of your father— the God of Abraham, the God of Isaac, and the God of Jacob." And Moses hid his face, for he was afraid to look upon God." (Exodus 3:1–6 NKJV)

Cheryl Williams—Bowen added, "He'll put His Signature on it. He's just good like that".

Visualize your season of singleness as a "burning-bush" experience before God. Did you notice in the passage that the bush was burning but it was not consumed? The bush did not burn up. The bush did not blow away. Why? It was because God compelled Moses to come to the mountain. When he did, he was on holy ground and assigned a holy ordained task! That holy ground God called Moses to was just for that time and for that need.

As you read this book, know that I, through the power of the Holy Spirit, declare this book as holy ground. I know God consigned this book to me. I was assigned and given this preordained task for such a time as this.

Singles (or whomever you are), take off your sandals (flip-flops, pumps, stilettos, kitten heels, ankle heels, booties, or wedges), or whatever of:

- attitudes

- doubts

- hatefulness

- fears

- anger

- remembering days of old

- remembering days of hurt

- remembering days of disappointment

As a single or whatever your reason for reading this book, note these scriptures:

- *Charm is deceitful and beauty is passing,
  but a woman who fears the Lord, she
  shall be praised. (Proverbs 31:30)*

- *The unmarried woman cares about the things
  of the Lord, that she may be holy both in
  body and in spirit. (1 Corinthians 7:34)*

- *But seek first the kingdom of God and His
  righteousness, and all these things shall
  be added to you. (Matthew 6:33)*

- *To everything there is a season, a time for every
  purpose under heaven. (Ecclesiastes 1:8)*

- *I beseech you therefore, brethren, by the mercies of
  God, that you present your bodies a living sacrifice,
  holy, acceptable to God, which is your reasonable
  service. And do not be conformed to this world, but
  be transformed by the renewing of your mind, that
  you may prove what is that good and acceptable
  and perfect will of God. (Romans 12:1–2)*

I feel the need to tell you why the Word of God is the only thing that will give us our wholeness. To be whole is to be complete. If something is broken, it is no longer whole. It is broken and it doesn't work. I read somewhere that something broken has the potential to be severely damaged. Hence, if you're recovering from a broken heart, broken situation, broken trust, you can often feel as if there's nothing that can fix it. It could cause one to feel less than—damaged beyond repair.

Dear One, the fixer is the Word of God and God's perfect love. I know you don't feel like it or maybe you're too busy, but spending time reading God's Word with prayer can repair the brokenness in your life.

When I say "His Word", understand I'm also saying, "With Him" because when your're hurting, He's with you. Because of my new relationship with Him, I've had to climb up on His lap, where He wrapped His loving arms around me and rocked me. Before that relationship, I did not know He was there crying when I cried and hurting when I hurt. I didn't realize He never left me. He was waiting for me to call on Him. He was waiting for me to reach out to Him. The microsecond I did, I felt Him! It was me and Him. Hallelujah! (I felt I needed to step up and share just then.)

Yep! He's there even when you can't see your way through. It is not just about the reading. I mean, shoot, you can just read a dictionary. It's about the relationship that's established through reading The Word:

- *We are hard pressed on every side, but not crushed, perplexed, but not in despair; persecuted, but not abandoned; struck down, but not destroyed. We always carry around in our body the death of Jesus, so that the life of Jesus may also be revealed in our body. (2 Corinthians 4:8–10)*

- *Do not be anxious about anything, but in every situation, by prayer and petition, with thanksgiving, present your requests to God. And the peace of God, which transcends all understanding, will guard your hearts and your minds in Christ Jesus. (Philippians 4:6–7)*

- *Come to me, all you who are weary and burdened, and I will give you rest. (Matthew 11:28)*

- *God is our refuge and strength, an ever-present help in trouble. Therefore we will not fear, though the earth give way and the mountains fall into the heart of the sea. (Psalm 46:1–2)*

And although you may think that you must follow some checklist for God to heal your heart. All He really needs is for you to bring your cares to Him today whenever your today with Him begins.

Enduring a broken heart can make you feel alone. It may make you feel that there's no one else who can really know what you're going through. The Bible reminds me daily and can assure you that no matter how broken you feel, God is always there to see you through. So if you need a bit of motivation or inspiration to get through your current heartache, doubt, or despair, here are a few ways to help you on your journey.

HOLD UP! BONUS SECTION

Where are your friends? Ladies, do you have friends that are females? Don't tell me "Yes, I have friends, but they're all guys." Let me quickly share this before we move forward.

When I was called to the ministry of women, I bulked. I (yep, I clapped back) humbly informed God those women were catty and combative. I followed up with I don't have the patience or the skill set to deal with that type of behavior and spiritual level. Yes, I had my small circle of friends that were females, but they were solid—my ride-or-dies! I never hung out with a lot of females. They got on my nerves—braggers, know-it-alls. I hated singles who were only out to find husbands (anybody's husbands), married women who were suspicious (like somebody wanted their broke husbands), and I couldn't trust either group. Now, the Lord was sending me into that field! Not this one. Those were the ones that lied to me, lied on me, laughed at me, made me feel less than, and now I was in a position to make a decision. Nope! Then I heard a still small voice, "But aren't you one of them?" Dag! He got me again.

Other than disobedience, I can't explain my hesitance. I have female friends. I call them my Circle of Seven (C7). Two ladies in my C7, when I met them, were married women. During our friendship, another one married and one divorced. The others were single women at varying ages. I don't go out and "make friends"; God sends them. I smile and am pleasant but very private and distrustful. When God established my C7, I worked with them in some capacity. We experience life together. We cried together, laughed together and were silly together. Bonds were built but that relationship was not built overnight. We invested in each other. Went through family trials and tribulations with each other. We were there when death came to parents, siblings and friends. Oh, I've had other "friends" other than the C7s but they were for a season and a testimony. When our season ended, so went the "friendships".

The C7 outlasted them all. Why? We kept our faith and our love of Jesus the object of our love and worship. Even though we all were a part of many of our decisions, He was the ultimate decision maker. My friends never became my idols. I never became their idol. I did not demand more from my friends than God intended them to provide. In other words, I never expected my human, imperfect sisters to be what God is in my life. Then they could never disappoint or hurt me and I could never do the same to them.

I found this outstanding article from Drew Hunter[1] (Wheaton, Massachusetts), who is the pastor at Zionsville Fellowship in Zionsville, Indiana. He wrote a couple of things I wanted to share about why God-ordained friends are essential in our season of singleness. He wrote, "We often treat relationships as consumers; we befriend for the benefits we receive. But like a contract, when the relationship doesn't give us the goods we want, we leave." He goes on to say that the Bible, specifically in the book of Proverbs, shows us that real friendship is more covenantal than contractual. Proverbs 18:24 teaches us about *"a friend who sticks closer than a brother."* It commands us in chapter 27, verse 10, *"Do not forsake your friend."* It warns us in chapter 19, verse 4

---

[1] https://www.biblestudytools.com/bible-study/topical-studies/what-does-the-bible-say-about-friendship.html, with additions from Rev. Linda Drumgoole.

about the fickleness of fair-weather friends: *"Wealth brings many new friends, but a poor man is deserted by his friend."* Pastor Hunter elaborates further with "I've never heard anyone say they wish for fewer, less-meaningful relationships. Each one of us longs to be more connected more deeply with friends. And this is because God made us for true friendship."

You don't have to be isolated. Singleness with others is or can be fun. I love being with me, but there is joy with other singles, married folks, and couples in balanced friendships. I felt the need to stop and share. Now are we ready?

Let's begin.

INTRODUCTION

This book was ordained and fashioned for everyone but intended for singles. Its contents are to aid in examining one's spiritual truth as a single. As Cheryl Williams-Bowen shared with me early one morning while chatting over a cup of coffee, "Drum, it's about peace and not pieces."

Is there a (secret) desire for someone to love and someone to love you back, but has that (secret) desire allowed you to lose yourself? This book's purpose is to draw out the hidden need of completeness founded on an individual's supposed feelings toward you. This book's intent is to unveil the love God has for you with no conditions, no strings, snippets, traps, or pauses of love but free unconditional 24/7 love!

Someone may say, "That's not me." I don't have those needs. Those (secret) desires! No?

ME. So why did you choose him?
YOU. Hmmm…because he makes me laugh.
ME. Girl, Bobo the Clown's job is to make you laugh, but can he make you whole?
YOU. (Crickets)

I dedicate this book to the lonely but not alone, to
the broke but not broken, to the picked on, and yes,
whom God picked out...for such a time as this!

Through our Wishes and Your Needs, we may believe
that we can solve our singleness if God would only grant us
our wishes. We know what we need, right? (No Dear One.
We do not but He does every time and in every way.)

THE DATE

*And you will seek Me and
find Me, when you search for
Me with all your heart.*
—Jeremiah 29:13

Each week, I received emails that annoyed me. The emails were
about spiritual quiet time or prayer time for husbands to their
wives or wives to their husbands. All of those were good, but I
saw very little or nothing about spiritual quiet times or prayer
times for singles or basic words of encouragement for singles.
Okay, so maybe I wasn't getting those types of emails because I
signed up for when I'm married. Hey, I needed to know how to
encourage my husband, right?

In my singleness, please understand, I need encouragement.
Some folks in this world can be hurtful and unkind, but
they cover it with their perception of "Christian Love". I've
experienced their modes of "love".

Those types of love caused me to run, fade in the background, or
stop serving in what I truly believed I was called to and where I
had passion and joy when serving.

Unfortunately, their type of love sent me to a place of being left
alone and isolated. Isolation causes you to slip away from the

Word of Truth. You begin to play the insolated and unhappy role of single and satisfied. Single and satisfied doesn't always work. Yes? No? Single and satisfied, in the church, has become a euphemism.

Are you single and satisfied? Do you ask questions like: "Where is satisfaction in the life of a single person? What do we do to keep from going down the pit of unhappy isolation? Folks tell us satisfaction comes during your quiet time, your study time, and your prayer time. It goes away when you're doing ministry or mission. But what about during the "Who am I?" and "What I ain't got?" time with the Lord? Where's my happiness? Where's my satisfaction? Why am I still in isolation? What did I do?"

I want you to know that I have discovered the answer. My answer is not a quick-fix spiritual diet that you lose the "You ain't worth it" or "This ain't my thing" and replace it with victories and hallelujahs for a month. Then in three months, you gain back double depression, disappointment, and dismay (triple gold with extra sprinkles).

My answer is the answer that will keep you for a lifetime. It keeps me, sustains me daily, and continually gives me victory even when the tempter, isolation or unhappiness tries to take me out! This solution will keep you current, consistent, and provide you with a lifestyle that is good for you and those around you! Interested? I mean what can you lose by trying my discovery? Think about what you can gain. Suspicious? Quick question: So what you have now is working? If so, stop reading and close the book or trust Jesus Christ and keep reading.

THE SOLUTION. This solution, believe it or not, is within God's plan for you. You might be thinking, should I or shouldn't I take a chance on this solution? I'm laughing. We will purchase or take chances when we're

in control or when we can financially attain it. You might
be hesitant because you're unsure if God's Will works.

You ready?

THE PLAN: A Step-by-Step Method to Wholeness

So here is what you need to do:

1. Make a date with Jesus. Yes. Make a date with Jesus.
    Crown or clown? Look, you've dated unsaved clowns,
    who on the outside looked good but caused you damage
    and baggage. You've dated supposed saved clowns
    and look at the wreckage, weariness and still wanting
    you continue to carry. So, why not Him? He won't
    stand you up. He won't look at you like you stank.
    He won't make you feel less than. He already knows
    you. He loves you intimately right where you are right
    now. The Bible says in Psalm 3:3a, *"But You, O LORD,
    are a shield for me, My glory and the One who lifts
    up my head."*[2] Why not Him? What can you lose?

2. Now ask Him. Try this: "Jesus, I need uninterrupted
    time with You. I want intimate time with You.
    Your Word tells me I should pray to You who is
    in the secret place. You, who see in secret, will
    reward me openly (Matthew 6:6-7) I desire to be
    made whole. Amen. "Was that so hard?" Now let's
    move forward to your first step to wholeness.

---

[2] Psalm 3:3 (NKJV).

3. Stop! Now on your smartphone, calendar, sticky on the mirror, or wherever you keep your important reminders, write down the date and time for the date. Don't schedule your date for next month. Don't wait to do it next week. Stop right now and schedule it for three days from now.[3] The number three is one of the most important numbers throughout the Bible. It is the number meaning harmony! It is a number of God's Presence. Three is connected to the Holy Trinity. It is connected with Jesus. He prayed three times before being arrested. He was put at the cross at the third hour of the day and died at the ninth hour which is three in the afternoon. The number three is the number of eternal life. Christ was resurrected after three days of being dead. The number three can be seen as God's power.

4. After you've made your decision, have a second conversation with Him. Pray "Jesus, I'm back. I have selected this date and this time. I will be ready. I look forward to spending time with You. Amen!"

5. Like all dates, you must prepare. Prior to the date, write down seven of your concerns, issues, or things that stop you from loving who you are today. Don't weigh them or think about them, but as they come into your mind, write them down. Stop at number seven. Take that page, fold it, and place it in your secret place. Yeah, you got a secret place. It might be in your Bible, top drawer, or wherever. Keep it there and prepare to bring your list on your date.

---

[3] http://numerology.center/biblicalnumbers/number3 modified by Linda A. Drumgoole.

6. When it's date time, dress for it. Get ready for Him. The God of creation desires time with you. Yes, you! You're worth it. Amen? Amen!

7. Where in your home are you going to spend time with Him? Select a place where you are alone with Him and only Him. Think about it as getting ready for Him!

8. Time has passed, and today is the day. The clock is ticking, and it's almost date time. Did you dress up? How did you dress? Did you dress in your heart and mind and not so much your clothes? This is the letting-go time! This is surrender time! Yes! This is your time with Him!

9. Seven minutes before the actual time, grab your list, a big towel, and a couple of boxes of facial tissue or a couple of rolls of toilet paper. It's your preference because you will need them.

10. It's time. Here is your awesome chance to talk to God. He's Abba God. Daddy. Don't get hung up here! Trust Him to be whom He has declared Himself to be to you according to His Word.

   Word to self: He's been desiring and waiting for this time with you also.

Let's do this.

*****

Begin by saying, "Hi. It's me, and I'm ready for our time today." Now just talk to Him. Begin by pulling out your list and reading it with commentary. Talk to Him. Release on Him. No disrespect but honesty. Tell Him about those things that might bring out anger. Tell Him your sorrows. Let go of your "less-thans." Don't blame or name anyone else. It's your unhurried time with Him. Go for it!

Word to Self: He's been desiring and waiting for this time with you also. He knows those hurts. He's been waiting for you to openly share your hurt with Him. It's the beginning of trusting Him.

Did you know this book was ordained for your benefit? It was written and declared specifically for you to make you better. Better is not bitter or blaming. It's letting stuff go—stuff you've held on to and at times stops you, lessens you, and causes you to settle instead of soar. That stuff that prevents you from breathing in the betterness ordained for you!

As you are releasing and if you are being real, you will cry. I'm talking about an ugly cry! I hear somebody ^ saying in a silly way, "I don't cry." While getting ready for this date, I asked you to write down seven of your most hurtful concerns, issues, things that stop you from loving who you are today. Those seven will bring up emotions and memories. Don't tell me you won't feel that brokenness again. You can't tell me you won't feel that sharp excruciating pain that caused you to weep and even now causes you to pause. So, Dear One, tears will come, so cry! Cry hard. Cry out loud. In fact, cry until you hiccup. When there are no more tears, wipe your face. Blow your nose. Say "Yes, Lord." (Come on, say it out loud.) Say it again. "Yes, Lord." Say it again. "Yes, Lord." Say it again. "Yes, Lord." Amen!

The date is coming to an end, but before you say good night, ask Him for another date. Yes. I need you to make plans for the second date before this date ends. Say "Thank You, Lord, for this date. I look forward to our next one." Be sincere. It's just you and Him. Tell Him you will reach out to Him tomorrow to schedule your second date.

Wow. Worn out? Better? A bit? On your second and third dates, I want you to add a new list. Go through and add extra to the first seven concerns. Go for it! On each date, when there are no more tears, wipe your face, blow your nose and say "Yes, Lord." (Come on, say it out loud.) Say it again. "Yes, Lord." Say it again. "Yes, Lord." Say it again. "Yes, Lord." Amen!

On the fourth date, after you go through your list, pause and spend time giving God thanks for who He is. How? Use at least three names that describe who He is for and to you. How are you supposed to know that? I got you. To me, daily, He's:

- Jehovah Jireh, "The Lord will provide" or "Jesus Christ My Provider";
- Jehovah Shalom, "The Lord Is Peace";
- Jehovah Rohi, "The Lord My Shepherd";
- Jehovah Tsaba, "The Lord Our Warrior";
- El Elyon, "Jesus Christ Most High";
- El Shaddai, "The Lord Jesus Christ Almighty";
- Elohim, "Jesus Christ the Strong Creator";
- Jehovah, "I Am Who I Am"; and
- Adonai, "The Lord Who Rules."

Now that's just a few. There are so many more!

Your dates with Him will begin to give you confidence in Him. Sharing your concerns caused you to trust Him. By knowing all that God is through His names, you will grow confident about who He truly is for you in this season of your life—your season of singleness.

Now, during your dates, begin to talk to Him about any and all things. By your fifth and sixth dates, I challenge you to list what makes your soul happy when you're using His names. On the seventh date, repeat. Don't get tired. Don't give up. In fact, make your dates enjoyable because of His abiding love for you. Then you will notice your relationship shifts with Him. You realize you don't have to schedule a date. Your relational communication with Him shifts from your head to your heart. Your chats are often, quick and immediate. You will have bad days. I promise you will find yourself speaking to Him about that "bad day" sometimes with just a whisper.

In preparation for your next date, note concerns or praises on your calendar to share with Him. There will be times when you may have to move away from others to pray for strength and encouragement. You will notice how your personal interaction with Him, for any situation or reason and at any time, moves to immediate comfort. Yes, Lord!

The Beginning of Your Former Conclusions

What happens during these dates as you experience Him (God the Father; Jesus Christ, the Son; and the Holy Ghost)? He becomes your joy, your peace, your self-worth, your spiritual growth, and your wellness. He begins to move you toward your recognized and continual whole. He demolished what was, redefines what is, and galvanized what will continue in you! He is the recipe for your victory! Can I get an amen? He got you!

You should now look forward to your time with Him. Due to your relationship with Him, you will confidently tell others about Him. They will see your difference…your wholeness.

"I want to know Christ— yes, to know the power of his resurrection and participation in his sufferings, becoming like him in his death" (Philippians 3:10)

HOLINESS

Blessed is the one who does not walk in step with the wicked or stand in the way that sinners take or sit in the company of mockers, but whose delight is in the law of the Lord, and who meditates on his law day and night.
—Psalm 1:1-2

God spoke to my heart the word Holiness. How did I know it was Him? My relationship with Him changed but this was different. I kind of knew it was Him, but I suppressed it. I made excuses. It must have been the wind I thought because I was told God no longer speaks directly…audibly. I ignored it and chalked it up to tiredness or "Just my imagination (once again)." It moved from my heart to my head and finally my ears. I kept hearing the word Holiness. At one point, I questioned my sanity. Of course, I didn't tell anyone. Who talks about a single word resounding in their heart, head and ears? The word began to infuse into me, and I was spurred to do something. That word halted me from moving in a direction that had been comfortable and safe.

I'd heard that word in church my entire life, but it meant little to me. Holiness was those folks up the street. Those folks who wore no makeup and long dresses.

Dear One, know that He wanted that word for this book. The word means "set apart, sanctified, consecrated." Ha! Those words sounded undoable in and for my life. How could I write about something that was so unfamiliar to me? Then I realized holy is what God is and He was calling me to it. Me? Holy? I wasn't anywhere near that. I'm so flawed.

I would cringe thinking I could never measure up to fit that criterion in no area of my life. Set apart? I don't want to be alone. Sanctified? I don't want to be known as that girl. Consecrated? Consecrated to do what? I'm teaching; ain't that enough? The evil one negatively influences my common sense of who I was and am in God. Holiness eluded me even though I knew God was calling me to holiness. I had no answer and therefore no peace.

I went to God's Word to find peace. 1 Peter 1:13–14 (Message) reads, *"So roll up your sleeves, put your mind in gear, be totally ready to receive the gift that's coming when Jesus arrives. Don't lazily slip back into those old grooves of evil, doing just what you feel like doing. You didn't know any better than; you do now. As obedient children let yourselves be pulled into a way of life shaped by God's life, a life energetic and blazing with holiness. God said, 'I am holy; you be holy.'"*

That passage was truly a lightbulb moment for me. It is so easy to "slip back into those old grooves of evil." We justify. We excuse. We accept. We ultimately mess up. With clarity, I stopped and prayed and immediately obtained peace. Why? How? I listened to the words of a song. The song is about my desire for holiness. The convicting words to this song simply declares, "Holiness is what I long for."[4] That's why I love this song. Here are the words:

Holiness, holiness is what I long for
Holiness is what I need
Holiness is what you want for me

Righteousness, righteousness is what I long for
Righteousness is what I need
Righteousness that's what you want for me

So take my heart and mold it
Take my mind, transform it
Take my will, conform it
To yours

Brokenness, brokenness is what I long for
Brokenness is what I need
Brokenness that's what you want for me

Wow. The doubt and negative influence fled. It's not where I am, but it's what I desired. I want to be what God already is even in my limited capacity. I'm striving daily to live a life that pleases Him. *1 Thessalonians 4:7 states, "God did not call us to uncleanness, but…holiness."*

As I am growing in Him, because of my desire to truly know Him, I find myself embracing holiness. How? It's because I'm spending more time with Him. Haha! We're dating! I'm excited about my quiet meditation times, date times, prayer times, study times, and my intimate alone times with Him. During those times, I'd stop to give Him praise and worship Him for who He

---

[4] http://www.songquery.com/html/title/t/take_my_life_vineyard_voices_scott_underwood_the_worship_leaders_series.html.

was in my life right now. He is the air I breathe. I can't and I won't be without Him. Holiness has become my lifestyle.

Look what I found: "Holiness does not consist in mystic speculations, enthusiastic fervors, or un-commanded austerities; it consists in thinking as God thinks, and willing as God wills. God's mind and will are to be known from His word; and so far as I really understand and believe God's word, God's mind becomes my mind, God's will become my will, and according to the measure of my faith, I become holy,"[5]

That says it all. As I spend more time with Him and in His Word, I hear myself sounding like Him, looking like Him, walking like Him, thinking like Him, and living Holy as "He is holy." Am I fully there? Nope. Far from it but I'm striving. To help with that, I've created a "Lord, check me" checklist:

- Are you spending quality time with God?

- Are you praying?

- Are you committed to personal praise and worship time?

- Are you reading, studying, and memorizing God's Word?

- Are you actively attending church?

- Are you attending a Bible-teaching church?

- Are you involved with other believers in your church?

---

[5] Adapted from Biblical Doctrine: A Systematic Summary of Bible Truth by John MacArthur.

- Are you faithfully involved in
  small group Bible studies?

- Do you have a discipleship mentor?

- Do you have accountability brothers-in-
  Christ/sisters-in-Christ partners?

- Are you using your gifts and talents
  to work in ministry?

- Are you being a friend to and praying
  for unsaved family and friends?

If you checked no in any area of the checklist, you are
susceptible to "slip[ping] back into those old grooves of evil.
The checklist is a gauging tool that supports and motivates
you to spiritually grow for His good. Think about it. Giving
up a former life of disappointment and pain, and you gain
_____(fill in all your gains). Stop and pray
this prayer:

Father, I offer You my heart. Take it and mold it. I offer You my
mind. Take it and transform it. I offer You my will. Take it and
conform it. I surrender it all for Your service. I want to be like
You, look like You, walk like You, think like You, and live holy
as You are holy. That is my desire. In Jesus's name. Amen.

As you move toward wholeness, know this: God is not concerned
with your happiness but your holiness. Happiness is fleeting. It
comes and goes. It's enabled when all is well. It fails and causes
scars when removed or snatched away. Holiness brings joy,
causes rejoicing, and magnifies your joy. Here are again some of
my scriptures of strength:

➤ *If you keep my commandments, you will abide in my love, just as I have kept my Father's commandments and abide in his love. These things I have spoken to you, that my joy may be in you, and that your joy may be full. "This is my commandment, that you love one another as I have loved you." (John 15:10–12)*

➤ *Though you have not seen him, you love him; and even though you do not see him now, you believe in him and are filled with an inexpressible and glorious joy, for you are receiving the end result of your faith, the salvation of your souls. (1 Peter 1:8–9)*

➤ *Nehemiah said, "Go and enjoy choice food and sweet drinks, and send some to those who have nothing prepared. This day is holy to our Lord. Do not grieve, for the joy of the Lord is your strength." (Nehemiah 8:10)*

➤ *Sorrowful, yet always rejoicing; poor, yet making many rich; having nothing, and yet possessing everything. (2 Corinthians 6:10)*

➤ *For his anger lasts only a moment, but his favor lasts a lifetime; weeping may stay for the night, but rejoicing comes in the morning. (Psalm 30:5)*

➤ *But the fruit of the Spirit is love, joy, peace, forbearance, kindness, goodness, faithfulness, gentleness and self-control. Against such things there is no law. (Galatians 5:22–23)*

➤ *Rejoice always, pray continually, give thanks in all circumstances; for this is God's will for you in Christ Jesus. (1 Thessalonians 5:16–18)*

> *Until now you have not asked for anything
> in my name. Ask and you will receive, and
> your joy will be complete. (John 16:24)*

Now when I hear the word holiness, I truly understand and embrace being "set apart, sanctified, consecrated." Ha! Those words sounded doable in and for my life. I now realize holy is what God is and He was calling me to it. Yep. This called, licensed, and ordained preacher is still flawed but striving daily to holiness! Can I get somebody to say "Yes, Lord?"

*He shall be like a tree
Planted by the rivers of water,
That brings forth its
fruit in its season,
Whose leaf also shall not wither;
And whatever he does
shall prosper.*

(Psalm 1:3)

EMPTINESS

Very early in the morning, while it was still dark, Jesus got up, left the house and went off to a solitary place, where he prayed.

—Mark 1:35

Okay, emptiness? According to my Internet search (because if it's on the Internet, it's got to be true, right?), emptiness is defined as "the state of containing nothing, void, vacuum, empty space, vacuity, gap, vacancy, hollowness, hole, lack, lacking meaning and sincerity; meaninglessness, quality of having no value or purpose; futility, loneliness."

That is so sad, and it might be true for others, but that does not define me. How about you? Right! Right! I ain't empty. I have friends. Real road dogs that are a phone call away. I work and have lots of folks around me. So empty just ain't me. I go to church. I have friends, brothers, and sisters in Christ who confirm that I am not alone. I'm not empty. I got stuff going on in my life. However, to be honest, I have and do at times experience spiritual emptiness. I experience it when I've made the wrong decision about a situation in my life.

Can you imagine a headache from eating chocolate, and you know you're allergic to chocolate? You take that "pain-away pill," and the ache goes away. You eat the chocolate which caused the pain, take a pill, and the pain ends. The pain comes from eating chocolate. It's in your power not to have pain, but you repeat it again and again and unfortunately again. The Bible says, *"As a dog returns to his own vomit, so a fool repeats his folly" (Proverbs 26:11)*. Oh my, the imagery.

It's not the pain that caused our trouble. It's the choice of choosing pain when we have the ability to not choose pain. By choosing pain, we have afflictions. Afflictions, torments, tribulations and woes. We see the flags. We ignore them. We justify the bad choices. We embrace the bad choices until the pain becomes so insurmountable. We then begin to complain, point fingers and blame others for our pain. Then we find ourselves running to Jesus. We attempt to hustle Him to take away our pain. Guess what? He ain't having it.

Literally, as I'm typing, God placed in my heart the story of Mary and Martha. Luke 10:38–42 says,

Now it happened as they went that He entered a certain village; and a certain woman named Martha welcomed Him into her house. And she had a sister called Mary, who also sat at Jesus's feet and heard His word. But Martha was distracted with much serving, and she approached Him and said, "Lord, do You not care that my sister has left me to serve alone? Therefore tell her to help me." And Jesus answered and said to her, "Martha, Martha, you are worried and troubled about many things. But one thing is needed, and Mary has chosen that good part, which will not be taken away from her." Was Martha trying to hustle Jesus justifying her tiredness, self-imposed martyrdom and her personal serve-a-tude status to Him?

He's in their home. Martha was distracted handling her business. In short, she chose afflictions, torments, tribulations, and woes. She (We) was so distracted entertaining, finding ways to make herself (ourselves) look good, and forgetting who's right in her (our) home. It's not like we can throw a stone at Sister Martha. Have we made the Master our priority, in our temple, and in our troubles?

Mary did. She sat at His feet and gained the "good part, which will not be taken away." When Jesus entered her home, Mary understood that right at that point and at that moment, He was her priority. Mary's desire was to be in Jesus's presence sitting at His feet. She had her priority in order. She did not embrace affliction but advantage, benefit, blessing, comfort, and delight.

We tend to be like Martha. We are worried and troubled about so many things. It causes our lives to be out of order. When we are out of order, we are just like that soda machine with the sign that indicates "Broken and out of commission"—not usable. We need to be fixed, repaired, and restored. Let's not get this thing twisted. God is not a "pain-away med" but a healer of the hurt that causes the pain. You've got to want to be fixed, repaired, and restored from the choice of choosing the pain. It's the trigger that desires the chocolate. It's folly. It's sin.

That's the point of our spiritual emptiness. We allowed unconfessed sin to move us from our strength. You can push that vacuum all day, but if it's not plugged into the source of power, it's just a broken and out-of-commission machine. How did we get unplugged? When did we get unplugged? Allow me to repeat. We allowed unconfessed sin to move us away from our strength.

How do you stay plugged into the source? How do you get your priorities back in order? How do you move forward, upward, and onward? How do you get rid of the spiritual emptiness that's taken up residence?

The Bible says in 1 John 1:9, *"If we confess our sins, He is faithful and just to forgive us our sins and cleanse us from all unrighteousness."* Confession is telling or snitching on yourself. Empty emptiness by spilling your guts on all that you have done. Anything that made you believe you are unworthy, no longer usable, and incomplete to walk in your calling. That's the trigger. Somewhere deep we have doubts about who we are and if we are worthy of our calling to serve. So, to squelch that inward turmoil, we move to something that gives us immediate relief. That type of unholy relief causes separation from our Holy God. The results: pain, afflictions, torments, tribulations, and woes.

When we confess our sins, He forgives and restores. He then will fill you up and supply you with everything you need to move toward your calling in Jesus Christ! You can't be spiritually empty if you're filled with the Holy Spirit, filled with the Word of God, and daily living a lifestyle of fulfilling holiness.

Here's more:

- *Sincerely desire the Holy Spirit's direction (Matthew 5:6 and John 7:37–39).*

- *Confess your sins (déjà vu) and give Him thanks (Colossians 2:13–15, 1 John 1:1–2:3).*

- *Give up control to Him in every aspect of your life (Romans 12:1–2).*

- *Confidently claim your wholeness according to His Word in Ephesians 5:18 and His promise in 1 John 5:14–15.*

Amen? Amen!

> *"I am the vine, ye are the branches: He that abideth in me, and I in him, the same bringeth forth much fruit: for without me ye can do nothing"*
> *(John 15:5).*

LIMITLESS

You want what you don't have, so you scheme and kill to get it. You are jealous of what others have, but you can't get it, so you fight and wage war to take it away from them. Yet you don't have what you want because you don't ask God for it.

—James 4:2

Once upon a time, a long time ago, my favorite shopping theme was limitless! The problem with my favorite shopping theme was my financial status. I was limited! That type of status renders it a necessity to budget or don't buy. Now, I'm that cash-and-carry or wait-for-a-discount kind of chick. My goddaughters Bri and Dani taught me to Groupon, RetailMeNot, and of course download all the stores with apps that notify me of sales! I budget and save to live comfortably. I must admit, I don't like that status and my new state of mind. It is a revulsion to my natural woman. I want, I desire, I crave limitless.

With my repurposed mindset might, I am happy, contented, and my life is balanced. I live on John 15:7, which reads, *"If ye abide in me, and my words abide in you, ye shall ask what ye will, and it shall be done unto you."* So when I go before Him, desiring anything, I know I'm under the protection of His love.

You might be saying, "Why do you do that? Don't you work? Don't you earn your own money? Don't you deserve limitless?" Allow me to tell you my story on how limitless caused me to move away from God's protection and into a world that came at me with limitless pain and limitless anguish.

It started for me when I thought I was a full-grown woman with the ability to make decisions and just do me. I was in my mid-20s to early thirties, making my decisions, loving the Lord, serving in ministry and relishing a sensible social life. A college graduate, living in Dallas in an apartment with a roommate. My costs were cut in half. I dated every now and then but mainly doing me most weekends. I had a good job with great benefits. Single with no kids, no pets, and no responsibilities. The Lord knew my heart, and forgiveness was available. I was covered. Can I get an amen?

I was traveling to Atlanta in the spring to shop. I showed up at events in New Orleans, New York, Washington DC, and anywhere I wanted to go. I traveled back and forth to Mississippi State University. I joined a sorority through their graduate chapter. I traveled to their events and purchased my swag to represent. I was eating out every day at high-end Dallas restaurants for lunch, dinner, and every now and then, while away, dining on Saturday and Sunday brunches of course. I was rolling with my church folks on Sundays, Wednesdays, and Saturdays when we had Bible studies and choir rehearsals. However, my non-church time was mine. My life was neat and balanced.

I went about life and kept busy with my twenty- to thirty-something-year-old friends who shopped like me until we maxed out our cards from our high-end stores credit cards. I paid the minimum and when I asked, they increased my credit limit. I told my friends, and they did the same. You see, they were my down girls who had fashionable hairstyles and nails. I even fell in love (lust) with several gents who meant me no good. The worst part was I knew it and knew better. I chose my clowns—my saved-in-the-church clowns, my rough-neck clowns, my businessmen clowns, my "we-just-buds" clowns, my in-the-world clowns, my traveling clowns. Yes, I saw warning signs, but I wasn't serious. I ignored them but found myself singing the circus music "doot-doot-doodle-oodle oot doot do do". I found myself in a circus state of mind pretending they were my crowns. False and fake contentment!

You see, the Holy Spirit was consistently calling my heart to yield, but shoot, I was still under destruction. Oops sorry, construction. I wouldn't listen. I wouldn't yield. I mean I was a full-grown woman and not a kid. I was just doing me. I was in my mid-20s to thirties and that's just what we do. Don't judge me. We all did it. Some of you are still doing it (no shade).

We all have at least four distinct lives: home or family life, work life, church life, and street or friends life.

My home or family life was safe and comfortable. I was invisible, and I stayed that way. I was an adult but was still treated like Lin. I was the chauffeur, the cook, the repair-buy-and-replace child, the housekeeper, the this and that, and whatever was needed child. I was so ready to leave when I went home. Please don't think me ungrateful. I loved my home. I loved my family, but this life was pressing down on the individualism that I craved. It took from my limitless mindset that sin awoke in my depth and made me callous and cold and unappreciative. I saw home at that time as a meaningless experience. My conversations were polite, respectful, but my heart was dismissive.

My work life was all about business. This was my bread and butter. I needed to learn all I could to move upward. I did not plan to stay years (that's a laugh because in 2022, I will celebrate thirty-six years). With a degree, I began at the bottom, and I've excelled up with a purpose. Now, I'm a supervisor with my eye on another position. I've expanded my vocabulary to learn their verbiage. No Southern twang. No Black-isms. No Chicago-isms. I'm educated and passionate. I've got to watch my aggression. Someone mentioned my volume. Shoot, I'm loud because I was born that way, but I can do that. No angry-Black-woman-syndrome label on me. My conversations will be sharp and knowledgeable, polite with substance, respectful with humor, and my heart with fake humility.

My street or friend life was on! This was the authentic me. Get that weave. Get those nails. Wait until the paycheck is in the bank. Pay that rent and the minimum on my bills. Let's roll. Makeup tight. Big girls need love too. Headed to Atlanta! Hair shows that include shopping galas. Was that wrong?

I always told at least 2 of the 7 that I was headed to DC or NYC but that's all. I never gave them an agenda. LOL! It's time to roll. With my pack, headed to Vegas to events asking, "we got tickets?" Later invited to the Superbowl in Miami and then off to a few after parties! I met so many folks.

"What's your name again? Dom?"

Dom to me: "Come see my suite."

My thoughts: Nope! Sister ain't stupid.

Me: "Too tired, so give me your number and we will talk and see."

My action: Crumble paper. Paper in trash.

My conversations would be shallow and uneducated; pouty; and always needy for food, fun and shopping; respectful with humor; and my heart with fake humility (but never giving my phone number or me to anyone). I told myself this was the way to filter out the clowns for my crowns. Sex was a no-no, but the appearance, the places, the conversations, the actions, all fell under the semblance of sin. The Bible shows in 1 John 5:17a that "all unrighteousness is sin."

My church life was a hot mess. The Lord knew my heart, and forgiveness was available, right? Like I said before, I was back on time for Saturdays and Sundays. Now let me make this plain, this was not every weekend. I only did this when that limitless sin gene presented itself.

Please understand I meant everything I did for God. The problem was He did not have all of me. He had bits and pieces of me. He had a bit of my time, a piece of my heart and mind, with none or a limited amount of my funds. Bits and pieces were all I was willing to give. Why? Because shoot, I was still under destruction. Oops sorry, construction. The Lord knew my heart, and forgiveness was available. Amen?

Then the world showed me what it had for me. My clowns clowned on me and juggled my heart with their unfeeling, uncaring, and unsaved hands. At times they tossed my emotions up in the air like balls and forgot, at times, to catch. The results of those clowns were the loss of my joy. I had serious credit issues and unhappiness. I ignored or changed my voice when debtors called. I became that non-English speaker ("She not here"). Where I worked, keeping my credit current was a major issue, and so I had to go to a credit counseling service. I had to make some severe and radical financial changes in my life. I eradicated some "friends and acquaintances" from my life. I cut up and consolidate all bills and bit by bit paid them off. I subjected and disciplined myself to a budget.

What's that? Joy? Something was missing. I no longer enjoyed my life. Things I did in the past that gave joy were gone. Then one day, at work, I heard someone say out loud, "I'm waiting." I went into my office, closed the door, and began to cry. I simply picked up my Bible (yep, a Bible in my desk) and went to Jeremiah 31:13, which says, *"I will turn their mourning into gladness; I will give them comfort and joy instead of sorrow."* Joy is true contentment based on faith.

That evening when I got home, I went into my room, and I screamed in my pillow. I didn't cry; I wept. I released my anger, hurt, disappointments, betrayals, and defeats. I cried out my confession of sins and my desire to regain my joy, reconnect with Him to cease my loneliness, and my commitment to serve in any capacity. I got up, washed my face, and took a deep breath. I looked in the mirror, and I smiled. I remembered Psalm 27:9 (NKJV), *"Do not hide Your face from me; Do not turn Your servant away in anger; You have been my help; Do not leave me nor forsake me, O God of my salvation."*

I knew that day that my life would never be the same. I looked at that new budget and realized my tithes and offers weren't included. I moved it to the top of the list. From my heart to my finances, I had to make Christ my priority. I looked at my smartphone and plugged in my quiet time so I would rise early and begin my day in personal prayer and Bible study. No more bits of my time, a piece of my heart and mind, with none or a limited amount of my funds. I surrendered all of me. I was no longer under construction. I was on a firm foundation of Jesus Christ. My heart was fixed. My mind was made up. I didn't know what He was going to do with my life. I didn't know where I was going to go or to whom He was sending me to, but I knew I was a hundred percent on board. Limitless in His love is the only thing for me. Hallelujah! Glory! Amen and amen.

I am the vine, you are the branches. He who abides in Me, and I in him, bears much fruit; for without Me you can do nothing. If anyone does not abide in Me, he is cast out as a branch and is withered; and they gather them and throw them into the fire, and they are burned. If you abide in Me, and My words abide in you, you will ask what you desire, and it shall be done for you. By this My Father is glorified, that you bear much fruit; so you will be My disciples. As the Father loved Me, I also have loved you; abide in My love. If you keep My commandments, you will abide in My love, just as I have kept My Father's commandments and abide in His love.

(John 15:5-10)

OH SHOOT!

God is our refuge and strength,
a very present help in trouble.
Therefore, we will not fear.
—Psalm 46:1-2a

"Oh shoot!" How many of you have said that phrase in your lifetime? Maybe you didn't say that word shoot but some derivative of it. My favorite phrases were:

- "Oh shoot! I messed up!"
- "Oh shoot! I knew it wouldn't work."
- "Oh shoot! Why not me?"
- "Oh shoot! Why me?"
- "Oh shoot! I can do better by myself."

And so forth and so on.

"Oh shoot" is frustrating and never a spiritual benefit for any of us. In the Urban Dictionary,[6] this is what I found: "Oh shoot!" is the phrase used in response to something surprising, awesome, or cool. It can also be used when an individual is excited or in shock at something. The phrase is also used when running into a friend in order to show an individual's happiness to see a friend.

---

[6] Urbandictionary.com.

That explanation fell short, so let's replace that meaning for "Oh shoot": onward, healthy, saved, humble, on-point, overjoyed, and tremendous.

Onward to God's plan for me.
Healthy in the Word and walk before me.
Saved forever!
Humble in knowing I was chosen to serve!
On-point with who I am in Christ!
Overjoyed knowing who He is to me!
Tremendous in the knowledge the Word is my barometer to holiness!

Let me share a story and my testimony. I couldn't confirm this scripturally, but this is my way of explaining this thing. Like Adam, God gave me a garden to tend. I will call it my faith garden. My job was to keep the weeds and bugs out of my faith garden and to keep my faith garden looking fresh, well-kept, and growing.

My faith garden contained all species of flowers and trees that nourished my faith and my faith flourished. I would rise early in the morning and do my God time, my quiet meditative time, my prayer time, my study time, as well as my intimate alone time listening. Then something changed. I began a harmless flirtation with an old groove thing.

What is an "old grove thing?" It's means to let loose and enjoy a carnal, nonbiblical lifestyle. Nothing sexual but sin-filled because I sometimes replaced my God-time with everybody else's time. This caused me to spend less and less time with Him, and less time in the upkeep of my faith garden. I talked or shared less with my friends of faith. I pushed back on my quiet prayer and Bible study times. The forever lifestyle I yearned became less important to me.

Spending less and less time with Him and hence my faith garden resulted in me spending time worrying about loneliness and disappointment. My "Oh shoot" (or a derivative of it) consisted of three areas:

1. Why don't I have male friends to hang out with and just have fun? Being lonely is not a benefit for me but a hindrance and an enticement to shopping! Since I don't have those male friends, I'm justified to stay out of my faith garden to find other things to do. (DECEITFUL)

2. Why don't I have that one male friend? I want that buddy to hang out with. Then the friendship grows to more and we begin courting. Then the friendship evolves into love for each other. Since I don't have that one male friend to grow into more with, I'm justified to stay out of my faith garden to find other things to do. (JUSTIFICATION)

3. Why don't I have a husband especially when I'm walking according to Your Word? I know women that have had not one or two but five husbands. Since I don't have my own husband, I'm justified to stay out of my faith garden to find somebody for me. (MANIPULATION)

Was my job really to keep the weeds and bugs out of a faith garden or was this just my imagination (once again)? (DOUBT)

That was my viewpoint! My "Oh shoot" (or a derivative of it) made me angry and fearful. I questioned my very worth. I questioned my beauty to others (doesn't anyone want me?). I worried I would be alone with nobody to love me into my old age. I smiled power and contentment on the outside and cowered on the inside. I limited God. I doubted Him, His love, His joy, His promises, and His ability to take care of my wants, needs, and desires.

During those times of doubt, to me, He failed me. He failed in knowing and caring about some basic needs for me His daughter. He failed to keep me and demonstrate (reward) His love to me. Hence, my garden was severely unkempt. I failed to water it daily, but when I remembered I would try to catch up. I did not have the correct tools because I was using those emails or texts "Verse of the Day" instead of a systematic way of studying the Word of God. I allowed bugs and weeds (sin) to enter and choke my garden. My beautiful faith garden became overgrown, unsightly with the appearance of being uncared and unloved.

Satan specializes in the seed of doubt. I allowed him and gave him entrance into my garden of quiet meditation time, prayer time, study time, my intimate alone time, and he planted that despicable seed of worry, loneliness, and disappointment. You see, I wasn't spending that vital quiet meditation time, prayer time, study time, my intimate alone time constantly. My oh shoots got louder and stayed longer. My faithlessness almost killed those precious flowers of peace, joy, and comfort.

The last time I felt the despicable seed of worry, loneliness, and disappointment, I stopped and prayed and opened the Word of God. It opened to the following:

But what happens when we live God's way? He brings gifts into our lives, much the same way that fruit appears in an orchard—things like affection for others, exuberance about life, serenity. We develop a willingness to stick with things, a sense of compassion in the heart, and a conviction that a basic holiness permeates things and people. We find ourselves involved in loyal commitments, not needing to force our way in life, able to marshal and direct our energies wisely. (Galatians 5:22–23)

That passage became one of my scriptures of strength. With my scripture of strength, I returned to my quiet meditation time, prayer time, my study time, my intimate alone time with Abba

God. The old grove got shelved and placed at the feet of my Father. I returned and began to tend my precious faith garden. My job was to keep the weeds and bugs out of my faith garden and to keep my faith garden looking fresh, well-kept, and growing.

Before I could restore it, I had to pull up the weeds. I confessed my remorse of unfaithfulness and doubt. I prayed for strength if those feelings returned and scriptures of strength I could lean on for power. I quickly returned and confessed to my friends of faith, along with my blood and blood-bought families. I shared with them my destructive path, thoughts, and ways. I realized I was not alone because many had been there, done that, and were restored. I was given grace to establish a prayer line and deeper prayer times at my church. My renewed faith garden sprouted new species of flowers, herbs, and trees. My faith was being nourished, and I flourished. As needed, with the power of praying hands, I pulled up the weeds and replenished the mismanaged soil. I faithfully dug up rocks, thorns and sharp thistles that appeared in my faith garden. I learned the battle was real and persistent but so was my commitment and surrender. With the renewed completeness from the Son (Jesus) and the vegetation (Word of God), my faith garden grew.

I returned to Galatians 5:22–25. It strengthened me more, and I saw the fruit of my faith garden. I saw the fruit of the Spirit, which is *"love, joy, peace, longsuffering, kindness, goodness, faithfulness, gentleness, self-control." Against such, there is no law. And those who are Christ's have crucified the flesh with its passions and desires. If we live in the Spirit, let us also walk in the Spirit."*

I retrieved and fortified my faith, and the door of doubt was closed, barred, and welded shut. Gone are the oh shoot:

"Oh shoot!" I messed up!
"Oh shoot!" I knew it wouldn't work.

"Oh shoot!" Why not me?
"Oh shoot!" Why me?
"Oh shoot!" I can do better by myself.
And so forth and so on. "Oh shoot!"

Enter the Oh shoot of:

Onward to God's plan for me
Healthy in the Word and walk before me
Saved forever!
Humble in knowing I was chosen to serve!
On point with who I am in Christ!
Overjoyed knowing who He is to me!
Tremendous in the knowledge the Word is my barometer to holiness!

Join me by saying, "Praise the Lord!"

"Come, behold the works of the Lord, Who has made desolations in the earth. He makes wars cease to the end of the earth; He breaks the bow and cuts the spear in two; He burns the chariot in the fire. Be still and know that I am God; I will be exalted among the nations, I will be exalted in the earth! The Lord of hosts is with us; The God of Jacob is our refuge. Selah"

(Psalm 46:1–8).

<u>VICTORIOUS</u>

Then God's peace, which goes
beyond anything we can imagine,
will guard your thoughts and
emotions through Christ Jesus.
Finally, brothers and sisters, keep
your thoughts on whatever is right
or deserves praise: things that
are true, honorable, fair, pure,
acceptable, or commendable.
Practice what you've learned and
received from me, what you heard
and saw me do. Then the God who
gives this peace will be with you.
—Philippians 4:7-9

Did any of you, when you were younger, feel you weren't really you? I mean did you ever feel that you were stolen or maybe a lost child from a wealthy family. I know, but go there with me for just a few moments, please. Did you have this inkling, suspicion, that you weren't born poor or born in that neighborhood?

How about feeling like you may have been kidnapped, lost, and found by others who made you drink a secret potion that caused your hair, skin color, and life to be theirs? How about feeling like maybe you were not born with that type of nose, eye color, body shape, or height? Any day, any moment, that door was going to open, and there would be a celebration. They found you. Victory and freedom will happen in your life! Sadly, you would wake up and realize it was just another broken dream.

Were you angry for a time and didn't know why? Had they forgotten you? Did they not know you were stolen, and somebody placed you there? Maybe you weren't born to be or do what you are doing now? Did you whisper in the night, "When is my time?" Then it happened! The big car would roll up, and this large bodyguard would escort you out. You would leave those rags and tags and broken toys. Then you would wake up. It was just another dream.

Those were a child's thoughts. You're an adult now. Reality has kicked in and it is what it is and there is no difference. There is no victory. You experience that chill. You experience déjà vu. That moment when you've felt that, you've seen that, and you've thought that. You hear that whisper, "When is my time?" No husband. Several husbands. Wrong husband. No respect? No dream this time. You're awake and everything is the same. You begin to believe victory is just a fable. There has been no victory, and there never will be one for you.

This chapter is for women who still are not comfortable in their being or essence—of their inner self. You love the Lord. Your worship is real. You stand on the Word of God. So why the sense that something is missing? You have a calling on your life, and what? You are not equipped. You are not prepared. Like always, it's the wrong number and it ain't for me.

You desire a victory. You want to win. You want the feeling or the ability to hold up your fist and say yes. Can you honestly say you have not had the desire for something to be about you? Who doesn't want a boost to their ego? In a place where you can lift your head and shout out loud, "It finally worked for me?" Bragging rights! Beauty accolades! Finest clothes. High balling. Shot calling. Three million followers and climbing on TikTok! I've had those feelings so many times. It's the desire of "my-will, making-it-completely about-me" syndrome.

Where is God's victory? The enemy continually inches in and negatively impacts one's self-worth. He tries his best to cause you to doubt your trust in God! Can somebody feel me?

When my victory happened it was not easy. How? I had to learn to surrender. Remember, I was a full-grown woman with the ability to make decisions and just do me. I was loving the Lord, serving in ministry, but my time was my time. He had bits and pieces of me. He had a bit of my time, a piece of my heart and mind, with none or a limited amount of my funds. Bits and pieces were all I was willing to give. Why? I was still under destruction. Oops sorry, construction. The Lord knew my heart, and forgiveness was available.

When I made the grown-up decision to step out of God's protection, yes, I was temporarily out of His protection, His fortification, His shield. I left Psalms 18:2, *"The LORD is my rock and my fortress and my deliverer; My God, my strength, in whom I will trust; My shield and the horn of my salvation, my stronghold."* Matthew 23:37-39 references God's protection withdrawing from Jerusalem. Verses 38 and 39 reads, *"See! Your house is left to you desolate; for I say to you, you shall see Me no more till you say, 'Blessed is He who comes in the name of the LORD!'"* Let me make this very clear. I knowingly and with forethought moved away from Him. It's kind of like that child that says, 'I'm running away' and the parent is driving the car behind that poor pitiful child while they are "running away". I needed to experience the consequences for my rebellious spirit against God. David said it best in Psalms 51:4a, *"Against You, You only, have I sinned, And done this evil in Your sight."*

When I walk out of God's protection, the world showed me what it had for me. I shared that experience with you earlier. My clowns clowned on me and juggled my heart with their unfeeling, uncaring, and unsaved hands. At times they tossed my emotions up in the air like balls and forgot, at times, to catch. I needed to go through some things; suffer some things and yes be reminded of some things. But God! Hallelujah. God reminded me that when I walked away, I left behind what was mine to pick up or rather take up. I remembered Ephesians 6:10-13 which reads, *Finally, my brethren, be strong in the Lord and in the power of His might. Put on the whole armor of God, that you may be able to stand against the wiles of the devil. For we do not wrestle against flesh and blood, but against principalities, against powers, against the rulers of the darkness of this age, against spiritual hosts of wickedness in the heavenly places. Therefore take up the whole armor of God, that you may be able to withstand in the evil day, and having done all, to stand.* I screamed, *"Blessed is He who comes in the name of the LORD!"* Then I stood up and surrendered. You've seen it on TV when someone surrenders. The one being arrested would raise up, hallelujah, their hands high in the air. They would then be placed into police custody.

Surrendering to God means letting go of your plans. It means letting go of you and allowing God to have His way in every aspect of your life to do His perfect will in your life. Some may see this as giving up, and yes, it is. Giving up sin. Giving up unproductive and destructive mentality. Giving up loneliness and self-doubt. Giving up what didn't work because you are finally giving it up to God! You see, being victorious equates to full surrender. Yes, you heard me! Being victorious equates to full surrender, full release, full trust in God!

I don't know why, but this dropped into my spirit:

Say "I'm yours" (3 times).
Say "Yes, I'm yours."
Say "I'm yours" (3 times).

When it appears to be hopeless
When it appears to be immovable
When it appears to be bottomless
You said, "Nope." It ain't. You caused me to turn around, sit
down, lift my hands, and say
"I'm yours" (3 times).
Yes, I'm yours
"I'm yours" (3 times).
When it appeared I was out for the count
When it appeared I had no way out
When it appeared I had given up
But then You whispered in my ear, "I'm here."
I knelt low, fell facedown, lifted my head, and said,
"I'm yours" (3 times).
Yes, I'm yours
"I'm yours" (3 times).
I'm saying "Yes."
I'm saying, "Order my steps."
I'm saying, "Use me."
I'm saying, "Restore my joy."
I'm saying, "Secure me, send me, yes, show me."
Because I'm yours
Now my vision is clear. I'm able to hear. I'm singing with joy.
My hope has been restored
You said, "I'm always near when there's doubt or fear
I've cried out, no more teardrops.
No more fight, I'm all sold out.
I'm raising my hands and singing again
I'm declaring my win, secured in Him
I'm yours (3 times).
Yes, I'm yours
I'm yours (three times)

When I finally surrendered, no more déjà vu or dreaming about my real identity. I was…I am a daughter of the King of kings and Lord of lords. I'm victorious because I know whose family I belong to right now. I'm in the right place, at the right time, to do the right thing, for so many, for such a time as this.

Now you? What are you willing to do? Be honest. Did you miss, stumble, or stopped doing something? After your first date, was there a second, or fifth date? Try it again, and I promise you, a relationship with Him gives life. Hebrews 13:5–6 reads, *"Let your conduct be without covetousness; be content with such things as you have. For He Himself has said, 'I will never leave you nor forsake you.' So, we may boldly say: 'The Lord is my helper; I will not fear. What can man do to me?'"* Amen? Amen!

"Whoever believes that Jesus is the Christ is born of God, and everyone who loves Him who begot also loves him who is begotten of Him. By this we know that we love the children of God, when we love God and keep His commandments. For this is the love of God, that we keep His commandments. And His commandments are not burdensome. For whatever is born of God overcomes the world. And this is the victory that has overcome the world—our faith" (1 John 5:1–4).

EXPIRED

*Do not conform to the pattern
of the world but be transformed
by the renewing of your mind.
Then you will be able to test and
approve what God's will is—his
good, pleasing and perfect will.*

—Romans 12:2

Done! It can't be used any longer! You gotta toss it out! It's expired! (While reading the beginning of this chapter, I want you to read it fast and panting. Only then can you experience and understand my heart during those times.)

Done! I can't be used any longer! Since I'm unusable like anything else in life, I've gotta be discarded, abandoned, rejected, removed, and/or tossed out! I've (sob) expired!

From elementary to middle school, I struggled. I didn't know why I struggled in school. If I heard information, I imagined and retained it. If I had to read something, I had difficulty retaining that information. My notes were good in my head. I would move the words from my head, and while writing the words, the meaning matched. Afterward, when attempting to read what I had written earlier, the meaning meant little to nothing. I could recall a bit of knowledge, but once I wrote it down, it left my brain. It was no longer there. Gone. My memory for that one topic, for that moment, had expired!

You might wonder, Where was my mother? She rose early in the morning headed to cook and clean in someone else's home. She left when it was dark and returned home when it was dark. Her love was undeniable. She trained me. I knew what to do. I never shared with her, even when she asked if all was okay, I never shared my hurt…my pain. I didn't have the words.

There were whispers about something that described my issue. My mom didn't know her loud, unafraid, bold child had difficulties when reading or saying certain words. She didn't know my other difficulties that ignited laughter from others. I taught myself how to say certain words correctly (Drumgoole Speech Therapy 101). How when I left early for school, I didn't bathe properly because the dryness of my skin burned. I didn't comb my hair properly because it was so tangled. I didn't sleep well at night and so I slept in school.

My teachers weren't aware of my difficulties. They weren't attuned to my struggles. No one called my home to ask any questions. My school counselors only asked about my college goals. No one ever called me to their office or asked me to stay after school because of my inconsistent grades. Did I really expect them to help me? In the back of my head maybe I hoped for a class on how to take great notes and retain information. Back then, maybe I hoped someone cared a bit to help or see me. Stupid me! You see, my date for expiration was fast approaching. I guess they could see my label, and so why bother?

Acting, writing, history, geography were my thing. Science was okay, but math or processing concepts were my weaknesses. I never allowed anyone to see those weaknesses. I learned to fake it. My memory was such that I did little to no studying, and remarkably, I could pass tests. That was only if I study that morning prior to the test. No time to discover why I saw letters or numbers out of order. I saw 798, but I read out loud 879. I would laugh about my errors. My note-taking was a mess. I would laugh off my messy notebook. There was no shingle in the school that read, "Let me analyze your note-taking that made no sense when you got home." Selah.

High School graduation! That time…done! That time…gone! The time for someone to discover my past issues. Can't use those sorrows anymore! You gotta toss those excuses out because they have expired! No more painful moments of mean kids, mean teachers, dismissiveness from folks who knew my address, my wood framed house and my lack of wealth. Here's a toast of celebration. That part of my life has expired!

Time to decide on which college, what degree? Any scholarships and grants? I heard the echo of two things: good job, good benefits. There was no real in-depth discussion on what to do or where to go. I thought to myself, "He [my brother Emmett] goes there, so it makes sense for me to go there." Did I finally make a decision that wouldn't make me feel like less than? Nope! Entry score not high enough. Summer program. Qualified! Accepted. I went there excited about a new start and a new me.

Oh shoot! The old me showed up. Nothing was different. My grades were barely passing. What's wrong with me? I'm intelligent. I can debate with the best of them. In most of my classes, I'm the only female. I'm not intimidated. The only African American. Not intimated. I study, but I can't pass those damn tests. I've got smart, skilled, in-the-stacks studying friends and I'm up there studying too but I'm too embarrassed to share with them my woes. Then when one professor attempted to talk to me about my grades, I had no words. No clue. I don't know me enough to articulate me.

I was active around campus. Party over here! I sang in The Black Voices of Mississippi State University. I went to church, and of course I knew the Lord, but I didn't know me. I didn't know where I fit in. I didn't know where I began, my middle, and my end. I dated. I had desires, but even that was off the table because I had no words, no clue. No future. No prospects. I was empty.

Yep, I graduated from college. Before I graduated, I discovered and attended classes that aided me in properly processing my thoughts and concepts. My writing and note-taking were organized and retrievable. I learned to read and reread everything I produced. I gained more confidence. As soon as I thought I was getting there, my time was done. The four years I just knew would redefine and clearly establish whom I was ended. It ended and couldn't be used anymore. So, what do you do with stuff you don't use anymore? You throw it away. You flush it down the toilet. You rinse the pot. You wait to see it swirl down the drain because it has expired!

I returned home. I taught school. I returned to my home church. I sang in the choir and became the choir president. I was active. I sang. I went to church, and of course I knew the Lord. I taught Sunday school. I bought a used car with no air conditioning. I had no wisdom. I didn't know where I fit in. I didn't know where I began, my middle, and my end. Then one afternoon I received a telephone call. My world changed. (From this point forward, I want you to read slowly and passionately. Only then can you hear and know my heart!) I was invited to come to Texas!

Immediately, upon arriving in Texas, God placed individuals in my life that affirmed me. It was like I was off that carousel of repetitive me and I felt for the first time that I could slow down to discover me. I began to believe that here, just maybe, I could get to understand myself. How? I rejoiced in the knowledge that if God had not divinely created His plan for me and had not caused that telephone call, I would never have discovered me. I began to hope that Texas might give me the promise of belonging. I hoped to discover my beginning, my middle, and my potential ending.

What changed? It was the folks God put in my life. Who and how? They did it by feeding my basic needs:

Spiritual. My best friend, Margaret, and her family attend Keller Springs Baptist Church. Pastor Willie Jacobs and 1st Lady Ozzie Jacobs were exceptional teachers. Their words and teaching consisted of: Repetition. Study. Classes. Methods. Madness. Craziness. Development. Church etiquette. Public speaking. Teaching. Rightly dividing the Word of Truth. There were many highs and lows, but my biblical foundation was firmly established. It wasn't about "what I thought" but what the Word teaches. I learned how to search the scriptures and strived to live them.

Emotional. My need to appear necessary (hair, clothes, makeup). God placed men and women in my life that affirmed me! They saw me. One took control of my hair care. Several taught me how to shop. I went from clown makeup to purchasing makeup to enhance and not cover up (I'm smiling while I'm typing). There were some tears. There were outliners who failed to understand the people God placed in my path. When they don't see you with males, they "ass-u-me." When you don't tell your personal business, they make up "s-tuff." There were occasions where they outright lied. However, none of it stung to cripple as it had in the past. Through the Word of God, I grew thicker spiritual and emotional skin.

Intellectually. I needed to know that I was smart. I could retain. I could pass a test. I wasn't dumb. My time in Texas affirmed my intellectual prowess. How? Opportunities repeatedly presented themselves. I was offered and attended gads of classes. Management classes. Management conferences. I attended training. I developed training. I taught. I did this not just for church but in the job God tremendously bless me to attain.

I became a biblical counselor. I completed the School of Ministry. Through the power of the Holy Spirit, I developed programs and protocols in church. I worked to positively impact others' lives.

One of my spiritual gifts is Discernment. That gifting allowed me to see what was on the inside of people that needed to be seen on the outside. He then trusted me with the gift of Encouragement. I grew in my faith. I excelled at work with a forward trajectory to higher heights. I began to realize that God's grace and mercy was for His glory. It gave me new testimonies to strengthen others. My beginning was revealed and confirmed, my middle was upward and onward, and my potential ending filled me with hope.

Then slowly but surely, all my siblings were getting married. I began to feel pressure from family and friends. "Lin, your childbearing years are approaching" was what I was told repeatedly. Let me be clear. First, hallelujah, I love men and I've never limited myself (race, color, shade) when it comes to them. Second, I've dated for years, but my family and the bulk of my friends never met them. Why? The clowns I dated weren't the One. When I tried to explain that to my family and those bulk of friends, they attempted to make me settle by saying, "You're just too picky," "Ain't nobody perfect," "You think you better than they are." Then the questions of my sexuality began to rise. "I wonder if she's gay." Really, friends and family? Really!?!? I had to remember God had a plan for me. He had a crown for me. I was waiting for His direction and His specific decision for me. To those who spoke into my life their plan for me, your're done! I can't use it anymore! It's time to toss their plan, their comments, their directions, and their assumptions out. For my life, God's plan will never expire. Hallelujah!

You know Satan is a counterfeiter, a swindler, and a crafty con artist (only listing a few). He does have the power to make us second guess, wonder, and grow weary. The Bible says in 2 Corinthians 11:3–4, *"But I fear, lest somehow, as the serpent deceived Eve by his craftiness, so your minds may be corrupted from the simplicity that is in Christ. For if he who comes preaches another Jesus whom we have not preached, or if you receive a different spirit which you have not received, or a different gospel which you have not accepted, you may well put up with it!"*

Their words penetrated, and it's true I weakened. Their words affected how I saw myself and my future. They spoke into my life the following:

- ✓ Go back to school? Higher education with your history of learning. Have you seen your college transcripts? You graduated, but, oh my, no graduate school will take you with those grades. Hey, you can't blame them.

- ✓ I know why you're not married. You don't have a husband because you won't give it up. When you buy new shoes, don't you try them on first?

- ✓ You know you suffer from lupus. That comes with limits. You know that, right?

- ✓ What's going to happen to you when you get old? You will be just another old woman, and you won't have babies to care for you.

Dear Ones, those comments hurt. Here's some wise counsel. If they (whoever the "they" are in your life) have or when they do bring to you their plan for your life, comments about your life, directions to make your life better, or assumptions on who you are at this point in your life, don't get mad at them. You see, the counterfeiter knows whom to use to get to us. Stop and remember my words of strength from the Word of God:

❖ *For God has not given us the spirit of fear; but of power, and of love, and of a sound mind. (2 Timothy 1:7)*

❖ *And they that are Christ's have crucified the flesh. (Galatians 5:24)*

❖ *For it is God which works in you both to will and to do of his good pleasure. (Philippians 2:13)*

❖ *But the fruit of the Spirit is love, joy, peace, long-suffering, gentleness, goodness, faith, Meekness, temperance: against such there is no law. (Galatians 4:22–23)*

You take those passages, and you stand. You stand with godly strength remembering who you are and who you belong to. Those passages remind me I'm not expired. I've got:

❖ Mary, Brian, Jerry, Carolyn, Emmett, Adrien, Jewel, and Cora—my siblings with their mates;

❖ Jack, Pinky, Leroy, Trevor, and a host of Drumgooles throughout the world;

❖ Brianna, Danni, Kendrick, and Marcus—my babies;

❖ Kevin, Sean, Aaron, Tasha, Rosie, and Emmett II—my strength and legacies;

❖ The Williams, Jacobs, Wilson, and Bowman Clans;

❖ My Keller Springs and Morse Street family—
  my God-ordained and blood-bought kin;

❖ My calling to preach the gospel of Jesus Christ with the
  power and might given to me for such a time as this;

❖ My work and ministry at the Morse Street
  Baptist Church (Where Jesus Is Lord).

❖ My work in the secular realm to be that
  light of the world, "*a city that is set on a hill
  cannot be hidden*" (Matthew 5:14); and

❖ Whatever and where else He has for
  me in such a time as this.

Me expired? You expired? Dear Ones, that's the biggest lie ever
told. It is imperative you seek, memorize and stand on your
scriptures of strength. Shoot, use all of mine in this book. Here is
one that you need if nothing else. It's Ephesians 6:10–20. I love
and live by it:

*Finally, my brethren, be strong in the Lord and in the power
of His might. Put on the whole armor of God, that you may
be able to stand against the wiles of the devil. For we do not
wrestle against flesh and blood, but against principalities,
against powers, against the rulers of the darkness of this age,
against spiritual hosts of wickedness in the heavenly places.
Therefore take up the whole armor of God, that you may be able
to withstand in the evil day, and having done all, to stand. Stand
therefore, having girded your waist with truth, having put on the
breastplate of righteousness, and having shod your feet with the
preparation of the gospel of peace; above all, taking the shield of
faith with which you will be able to quench all the fiery darts of
the wicked one. And take the helmet of salvation, and the sword
of the Spirit, which is the word of God; praying always with all*

prayer and supplication in the Spirit, being watchful to this end with all perseverance and supplication for all the saints and for me, that utterance may be given to me, that I may open my mouth boldly to make known the mystery of the gospel, for which I am an ambassador in chains; that in it I may speak boldly, as I ought to speak. (Ephesians 6:10–20)

I've changed expired with the word inspired! His love is everlasting without end or beginning. Hallelujah! Glory!

"Do not be anxious about anything, but in every situation, by prayer and Do your best to present yourself to God as one approved, a worker who does not need to be ashamed and who correctly handles the word of truth"

(2 Timothy 2:15).

DEPORTMENT

Turn my heart toward your statutes and not toward selfish gain. Turn my eyes away from worthless things; preserve my life according to your word.

—Psalm 119:36-37

On every page of this book, I've not thrown shade (expression of contempt for or disgust with) on anyone. I've been led to write this book because of how God had to work (and still is) some things out of me as well as into me. He then led me to understand I'm not the only one going through. However, this is an area that I struggle with even now. I have an issue with this topic: deportment.

Deportment is the last chapter in this book for a reason. This chapter took the longest to write. I cried more with this chapter. I struggled more with this chapter. My hands and head hurt more with this chapter. I was chastised by God more because of my rebellious spirit with this chapter. I agonized, walked away, and deleted this chapter from the book. I gave it several names, but not one was the right one. I finally surrendered and eventually was so blessed and healed at the end of writing this chapter.

Did you know deportment has fifty-seven synonyms? Fifty-seven ways to restrain yourself and teach yourself how to behave. Fifty-seven ways on how to present yourself, be polite, well-dressed, and soft-spoken. It speaks to how one should dress, look, and carry oneself in all parts of demeanor. If one is helpful and smiles a lot, if one is friendly and kind, they are exhibiting proper deportment.

Deportment is about my performance, my mode of behaving, my way of acting, and my way of conducting myself. It's about my etiquette, habits, practices, actions, acts, activities, and exploits.

This world has rules governing my deportment in and out of my job, church, and the public. The reason I have an issue with this word is that I'm supposed to do my best even when I'm talked about, hated on, lambasted, laughed about, let down, and disappointed. I'm supposed to smile when I'm judged by my color, hair, size, weight, look, style, fashion, where I shop, where I don't shop, and who I am not.

My natural is to retaliate, get snippy, throw deep resounding shade, and do it as a joke (jabbing, odious, knifing with empty emotions), or unload. I just felt you. Somebody just whispered or thought, "You are the preacher? Why didn't you go to the Word?" Yeah, I know what the Word says especially in the book of Romans. Romans 12 says:

- *"If it is possible, as much as depends on you, live peaceably with all men" (verse 18).*

- *"Repay no one evil for evil" (verse 17).*

- *"Bless those who persecute you; bless and do not curse" (verse 14).*

- *"Present your bodies a living sacrifice, holy, acceptable to God, which is your reasonable service" (verse 1).*

- *"Abhor what is evil" (verse 9).*

Amen!

What if:

- I'm tired of applying the balm of the Word on parts of my body abused by others.

- I want to react and fight back because of my place, position, and power of decision.

- My tear ducts are infected because I've held back the tears that stung my heart and soul because someone's boldness gave them privilege to (politely) offend.

You see, I'm one of those sisters who had to learn how to express love openly. In my family, you are guilty and must prove yourself innocent. It became a shield to keep me safe. To null the pain from others' cruelty. Then I grew up and I had to learn how to function with the shield. With non-family or close friends, I had to learn to speak cordially to everyone. I had to learn to be kind even when I wasn't feeling it. The shield grew larger, taller, heavier, and I used it flawlessly. I had no heart love. It was only fake-functioning head love. Then God moved.

When moving to Texas, my deportment lessons developed me spiritually, emotionally, and intellectually. The shield began to shatter, but I kept pieces of it. I tried to push forward to do right "but pressure," as Marian Horne once told us, "Will cause a pipe to burst." The Bible (Romans 7:17–25 Message) explains it this way:

But I need something more! For if I know the law but still can't keep it, and if the power of sin within me keeps sabotaging my best intentions, I obviously need help! I realize that I don't have

what it takes. I can will it, but I can't do it. I decide to do good, but I don't really do it; I decide not to do bad, but then I do it anyway. My decisions, such as they are, don't result in actions. Something has gone wrong deep within me and gets the better of me every time. It happens so regularly that it's predictable. The moment I decide to do good, sin is there to trip me up. I truly delight in God's commands, but it's pretty obvious that not all of me joins in that delight. Parts of me covertly rebel, and just when I least expect it, they take charge. I've tried everything and nothing helps. I'm at the end of my rope. Is there no one who can do anything for me? Isn't that the real question? The answer, thank God, is that Jesus Christ can and does. He acted to set things right in this life of contradictions where I want to serve God with all my heart and mind but am pulled by the influence of sin to do something totally different. (Romans 7:17–25 Message; italics added)

When God's Word simplified it, I got it. I realized I don't have the capacity to keep myself at bay. My natural man, the Drumgoole in me, does not have the ability to conduct myself to the standard that God desires. This caused the natural me to create a shield, a callus to harden my heart, mind, and ability to truly love with an open heart. Old scars, hurts, and wounds had marred me, and my self-created shield would allow no one to get that opportunity again. Then came the Word, the Word of God. I began a fresh and strong relationship with Him.

"His Word" was "Him." When I hurt, He was there. I remember the first time I climbed up on His lap, and He rocked me. When I cried, He cried. When I hurt, He hurt. He never left me. I began to understand my worth in Him. It began to take root. The pieces of shield I kept melted away without a scar or residue. I wanted; I desired to change. My performance, my mode of behavior, my way of acting, and my way of conducting myself took on a swag that made me feel better about the person I was becoming in

Christ. It didn't matter what folks thought. It mattered how I was carrying myself, deporting myself as His daughter.

I made my life about my etiquette, habits, practices, actions, acts, activities, and exploits in Him through the power and guidance of the Holy Spirit. That still small voice reminded me[7] God is:

- The Omnipotent God who is all-powerful;

- The Immutable God who cannot change;

- The Holy God who is separate
  from sin and incorruptible;

- The Aseity God who is so independent
  that He does not need us (me);

- The Impeccability God who is unable to sin;

- The Incorporeal or Spiritual God who is a Spirit;

- The Incomprehensible God, meaning
  He is not able to be fully known;

- The Good God who is the final standard of good,
  and all that He is and does is worthy of approval;

- The Eternal God who existed beyond time;

- The Omniscient God who is all knowing; and

- The Oneness or Unity of God who is the one and only.

---

[7] .https://en.wikipedia.org/wiki/Attributes_of_God_in_Christianity.

The Holy Spirit then moved me to Ephesians 6:12–18. I need you to stop, take your time, and really read this:

And that about wraps it up. God is strong, and he wants you strong. So take everything the Master has set out for you, well-made weapons of the best materials. And put them to use so you will be able to stand up to everything the Devil throws your way. This is no afternoon athletic contest that we'll walk away from and forget about in a couple of hours. This is for keeps, a life-or-death fight to the finish against the Devil and all his angels. Message (Ephesians 6:12–18)

I found myself returning to Romans 12 and meditating on:

- *"Do not be wise in your own opinion" (verse 16).*

- *"And do not be conformed to this world, but be transformed by the renewing of your mind, that you may prove what is that good and acceptable and perfect will of God" (verse 2).*

- *"Beloved, do not avenge yourselves, but rather give place to wrath; for it is written, 'Vengeance is Mine, I will repay,' says the Lord" (verse 19).*

I returned to the Attributes of God and remembered the Sovereignty of God. He was, He is, He will always be the supreme authority, and I humbly bowed to the realization that all things are under His control. So, in or out of anything I do, I had to humble myself and carry myself in a manner that glorifies God.

My deportment reflected who He is in my life—my life that I surrendered to Him so long ago. When those emotions show themselves, and they do and will, I remember that "greater is He that is in me that he that is in the world." I have to remember that I am of God.

I daily, painstakingly, dress with Ephesians 6:13–18:

The whole armor of God, that you may be able to withstand in the evil day, and having done all, to stand. Stand therefore, having girded your waist with truth, having put on the breastplate of righteousness, and having shod your feet with the preparation of the gospel of peace; above all, taking the shield of faith with which you will be able to quench all the fiery darts of the wicked one. And take the helmet of salvation, and the sword of the Spirit, which is the word of God; praying always with all prayer and supplication in the Spirit, being watchful to this end with all perseverance and supplication.

I now find joy in the opportunity to share even when I'm not feeling it. I carry myself no longer as a target but as a servant. My deportment now becomes a privilege and pleasure for the moments when I can tell my story that leads others to His story. Only then can He use my wholeness! Amen.

"'For I know the thoughts that I think toward you,' says the Lord, 'thoughts of peace and not of evil, to give you a future and a hope.' Then you will call upon Me and go and pray to Me, and I will listen to you. And you will seek Me and find Me, when you search for Me with all your heart"
(Jeremiah 29:11–13).

Note from Me

If you take the first letter of each chapter you get "The Loved."
The Loved means to love someone with the love poured out
into our hearts by the Holy Spirit. Our own imperfect love fails,
fades, ebbs, and flows as we grow tired, hungry, go through pain
and sorrow, good times and bad. God's love is always *"patient,
kind, doesn't envy, is never jealous, never arrogant, or rude, and
it can never fail. It bears all things, believes all things, hopes all
things, endures all things"* (1 Corinthians 13:4d-7). Drawing on
His knowledge gives us what we do not have naturally within
ourselves. This "thang" is supernatural.

Telling someone that we love them in Christ (which is a
reference to the presence of the Holy Spirit) means we are
admitting that the relationship isn't held together by our own will
and emotions but by our Father's Gift of Grace—His Holy Spirit.

I wrote this book because I needed to tell my story of healing and
wholeness because of my own healing and continuing wholeness.
What about you? It's time. It's time for every part of you to be
made whole.

ASS: A SERVING SISTER JOURNEY

As I end this book, let me add my story. I assure you I never asked for this life nor this path. I've heard it read and preached all my life, and I've read, researched, and studied it for myself.

Let your women keep silent in the churches, for they are not permitted to speak; but they are to be submissive, as the law also says. And if they want to learn something, let them ask their own husbands at home; for it is shameful for women to speak in church. (1 Corinthians 14:34–35)

Amen.

I've also heard it read and preached all my life, and I've read, researched, and studied it for myself.

Let a woman learn in silence with all submission. And I do not permit a woman to teach or to have authority over a man, but to be in silence. For Adam was formed first, then Eve. And Adam was not deceived, but the woman being deceived, fell into transgression. Nevertheless, she will be saved in childbearing if they continue in faith, love, and holiness, with self-control. (1 Timothy 2:11–15)

Amen.

While pondering the validity of my calling, I was moved to a
story in Numbers 22:19-29:

LORD will say unto me more.

*And God came unto Balaam at night, and said unto him, "If the
men come to call thee, rise up, and go with them; but yet the
word which I shall say unto thee, that shalt thou do. And Balaam
rose up in the morning, and saddled his ass, and went with the
princes of Moab."*

*And God's anger was kindled because he went: and the angel
of the Lord stood in the way for an adversary against him. Now
he was riding upon his ass, and his two servants were with him.
And the ass saw the angel of the Lord standing in the way, and
his sword drawn in his hand: and the ass turned aside out of the
way and went into the field: and Balaam smote the ass, to turn
her into the way. But the angel of the Lord stood in a path of the
vineyards, a wall being on this side, and a wall on that side. And
when the ass saw the angel of the Lord, she thrust herself unto
the wall, and crushed Balaam's foot against the wall: and he
smote her again.*

*And the angel of the Lord went further, and stood in a narrow
place, where was no way to turn either to the right hand or to the
left. And when the ass saw the angel of the Lord, she fell down
under Balaam: and Balaam's anger was kindled, and he smote
the ass with a staff. And the Lord opened the mouth of the ass,
and she said unto Balaam, "What have I done unto thee, that
thou hast smitten me these three times?" And Balaam said unto
the ass, "Because thou hast mocked me: I would there were a
sword in mine hand, for now would I kill thee."*

*And the ass said unto Balaam, "Am not I thine ass, upon which
thou hast ridden ever since I was thine unto this day? Was I ever
wont to do so unto thee?" and he said, "Nay." Then the Lord*

*opened the eyes of Balaam, and he saw the angel of the Lord
standing in the way, and his sword drawn in his hand: and he
bowed down his head and fell flat on his face. And the angel of
the Lord said unto him, "Wherefore hast thou smitten thine ass
these three times? Behold, I went out to withstand thee, because
thy way is perverse before me: And the ass saw me and turned
from me these three times: unless she had turned from me, surely
now also I had slain thee, and saved her alive." And Balaam said
unto the angel of the Lord, "I have sinned; for I knew not that
thou stoodest in the way against me: now therefore, if it displease
thee, I will get me back again." (Numbers 22:20–29)*

Amen.

Please don't read this as flippant. I don't believe God shared this
with me so long ago to offend anyone but to assure me of my
calling. Please see me as an ASS (A Serving Sister). God has
called me as a serving sister in Christ to share the Word of God
to all going down the path or road of sin and death.

The Book of Numbers reads, *"The Lord opened the mouth of the
ass, and she said, "And hence I open my mouth."* To all reading
this book, know this, I was called to open my mouth and speak
God's truth. As an opportunity presents itself, I open my mouth
to share the gospel that turns them away from the road of sin and
death to life eternal in Christ.

First, their need to be saved. The Bible in Romans 3:23 says
that all have sinned. Romans 6:23 says, *"The wages of sin is
death."*

Second, the assurance that they can be saved. Because of
Jesus's death on the cross, you can be saved. Romans 5:8 says,
*"But God demonstrates His own love toward us, in that while we
were still sinners, Christ died for us."*

Third, what they need to do to be saved. Romans 10:9–10 says, *"If you confess with your mouth the Lord Jesus and believe in your heart that God has raised Him from the dead, you will be saved. For with the heart one believes unto righteousness, and with the mouth confession is made unto salvation."* This leads us to Romans 10:13, which says, *"Whoever calls on the name of the Lord shall be saved."*

My calling and voice journeys only to those that will hear.

Epilogue

⚓ Are you ready?

⚓ Did conviction happen as you read this book?

⚓ Did your walk, while reading this book, cause you to turn around and go on a new and God-designed path?

⚓ If you are saved, are you walking toward sanctification: to be set apart, designed for a sacred purpose?

⚓ Have you or are you ready to be set apart, made holy as a vessel, full of the Holy Spirit for God's glory?

⚓ Are you watching for deceivers, counterfeiters, swindlers, crafty con artists, and clowns understanding that all the treasures of wisdom and knowledge are hidden and discoverable in Him?

Yes? It's time to go on that special date like the man with leprosy in Luke 17:15–19:

And one of them, when he saw that he was healed, turned back, and with a loud voice glorified God, and fell down on his face at his feet, giving him thanks: and he was a Samaritan. And Jesus answering said, "Were there not ten cleansed? But where are the nine? There are not found that returned to give glory to God, save this stranger." And he said unto him, "Arise, go thy way: thy faith hath made thee whole." (Luke 17:15–19)

Stop! Right now! Go back and read it again: Luke 17:11–19.

During your date, glorify God, fall on your face, and give Him thanks for who He is in your life. He has made you whole! You are no longer broken. You are complete. You are well.

SHARING LIFE ETERNAL

You've read this book, but maybe you've never accepted Jesus Christ as Savior or maybe you have walked away from the cross of salvation for whatever reason. Know this: God loves you and wants you to experience the peace and life He offers. The Bible says, *"For God so loved the world that He gave His only begotten Son, that whoever believes in Him should not perish but have everlasting life" (John 3:16)*. He has a plan for you.

We were all separated from Him. The Bible says, *"For all have sinned and fall short of the glory of God" (Romans 3:23). God is holy, but we are human and don't measure up to His perfect standard. We are sinful, and "the wages of sin is death" (Romans 6:23).*

God's love bridges the gap of separation between you and Him. When Jesus Christ died on the cross and rose from the grave, He paid the penalty for your sins. The Bible says, " 'He Himself bore our sins" in His body on the cross so that we might die to sins and live for righteousness; "By His wounds you have been healed" (1 Peter 2:24).

You cross the bridge into God's family when you accept Christ's free gift of salvation. If you are not a believer or have never invited Jesus Christ into your life:

- First, you must understand your need to be saved. The Bible says that due to sin, you need to be saved. Romans 3:23 and 6:23 say that *"all have sinned, and the wages of sin is death."*

- Second, you must understand you can be saved. Because of Jesus's death on the cross, you can be saved. Romans 5:8 says that *"But God shows his love for us in that while we were still sinners, Christ died for us."*

- Third, you must understand what you need to do to be saved. Acts 3:19 says, *"Now it's time to change your ways! Turn to face God so he can wipe away your sins, pour out showers of blessing to refresh you, and send you the Messiah he prepared for you, namely, Jesus."*

- Lastly, you must act if you want to be saved. Romans 10:13 says that *"anyone that calls upon the name of the Lord shall be saved."*

If you are ready to trust Christ as your Savior, repeat after me:

Dear Lord Jesus. I know I am a sinner. I know you died for my sins. Right now, I invite you into my heart to be my Savior and Lord. I willingly turn away from my sins and give my life to you. Thank you for saving me. Amen

Welcome to the family of God.

Finally, Revelation 3:20–22 reads, *"Behold, I stand at the door and knock. If anyone hears My voice and opens the door, I will come in to him and dine with him, and he with Me. To him who overcomes I will grant to sit with Me on My throne, as I also overcame and sat down with My Father on His throne. He who has an ear, let him hear what the Spirit says to the churches."*

I'm always concerned for those believers who walked away. Some words used to explain them as backslidden, unrepentant believers who, in their self-sufficiency excluded the risen Lord from their personal lives and concluded He's not necessary. That is more than likely true but I've witnessed how church folks demonstrated ungodly behavior towards them.

In fact, they've made new and even seasoned believers feel unwelcome. They've, in essence, have shown them the door when they've fallen instead of grace or mercy. The backslidden found more love and grace from non-believers and made the decision to turn from their faith, stay out of the church and never return. When I've run across individuals with that heart, they share their story with me. They confess their willingness to even return but shame kept them out but more importantly, nobody looked for them.

Church folks turned their backs on them and weren't out there like the prodigal son's Dad (Luke 15:11–32) waiting for his child to return home. I tell myself (never them), "Come on, let's be fair." I've seen folks abused and cheated in all types of stores, establishments, that include non-Christian folks. They chose not to return to that particular store, establishment, or non-Christian person, but they continue with life and find others.
The church, filled with regular, everyday humans, is where backslider are inclined to just give up on. That's why faith is an individual action. It's between you and Jesus Christ.
Well, today, in His expression of love, Jesus asks permission today to reenter and reestablish fellowship with you. Today, if you are reading this book, it wasn't by chance. God's invitation today to you, is to establish a second, third, fourth, hundredth chance with Him. It's never too late. I told you earlier. He never left. He's right there. Today, stop, turn around and call out to Him.

Here is where I find myself repenting my spiritual half-heartedness, my spiritual hard-headedness, my need to control and promote my personal agenda. Here is where I must willingly drop the attitude and accept His Will and His Agenda for my life. Is there anyone reading this book that can raise your hand and say, "I concur?" This is the place where I fall in and will continually fall in and work until I'm called home. What you wanted was an immediate love, but it was denied by man.

He's calling you today to allow Him entrance so you can fulfill what was designed by Him as He does His part for your restoration and your good. He's giving you that chance daily, hourly, moment by moment, and yes, second by second. I've learned in some areas and learning in others to embrace the passage, *"Trust in the Lord with all your heart, and lean not on your own understanding; In all your ways acknowledge Him, and He shall direct your paths"* (Proverbs 3:5–6). Jesus is ready with arms extended to you another chance…a better chance… the only right chance. You have nothing to lose but so much to gain. If you are ready to trust Christ and return to Him, pray this prayer:

Precious Father, my spirit is weak. By choosing sin, I have gone far from You. I've strayed and don't know how to return or too embarrassed to return. I have sinned against You God and you alone. I realize now that I need You more than ever and I want, I'm ready to come back to You. Forgive me. Refresh and renew me with Your grace. Amen. Hey!!! WELCOME BACK HOME with Psalms 51:12, *"Restore to me the joy of Your salvation, And uphold me by Your generous Spirit."*

I've learned in some areas and learning in others to embrace the passage, *"Trust in the Lord with all your heart, and lean not on your own understanding; In all your ways acknowledge Him, and He shall direct your paths"* (Proverbs 3:5–6). My last words to you: If you take the first letter of each chapter you get "The Loved." The Loved is you. I challenge you to go out and love someone with the love Christ poured out into your heart by the power of the Holy Spirit today and forever. Be blessed! Amen.

ABOUT THE AUTHOR

 Reverend Linda A. Drumgoole is actively serving the Lord at the Morse Street Baptist Church (Where Jesus Christ is Lord) as an Assistant Minister, the Director of Christian Education and Fellowship Ministries. She is a graduate of CTI's (Covenant Training Institute) School of Ministry at the Covenant Church. She is a certified Biblical Counselor from Southwestern Baptist Theological Seminary. Reverend Drumgoole has a Bachelor of Arts degree in Political Science from Mississippi State University and a Masters of Management from the University of Phoenix. Twenty-four years of experience in alternative dispute resolution and certified in conflict resolution for religious organizations. Finally, she is an active member of Alpha Kappa Alpha Sorority, Incorporated.

Printed in the USA
CPSIA information can be obtained
at www.ICGtesting.com
LVHW021606291123
764735LV00005B/28